ARS MINOTAURICA

Carey Scott Wilkerson
Poems

Copyright© Carey Scott Wilkerson, 2012

Copyright Cover Art© Joshua Jarrett, 2012

Copyright Cover Design© Melissa Dickson, 2012

Printed in the United States of America

All Rights Reserved

Library of Congress Control Number 2012947053 ISBN

978-0-9857703-1-0

Ars Minotaurica, by Carey Scott Wilkerson

Published by Summerfield Publishing, New Plains Press

PO Box 1946

Auburn, AL 36831-1946

Newplainspress.com

*Now, whether all this is by means of images
or not, who can rightly affirm?*

~ St. Augustine

for Tara and Pixie and the poetry of your lives…

TABLE OF CONTENTS

Part One

Felix with Toolkit	9
Dream of the Labyrinth Semiotician	11
Minotaur's Open Letter to Ovid	13
Minotaur finds a Mirror	14
Pasiphaë with Baby Minotaur	15
Minotauric Equiviocations With Shattered Referent Machine	16
Five Minotauric Motivics	18
Displacement Theory Song	19
Ariadne's Skeptical Daydream	21
l'infamïa di Creti	22

Part Two

Seven Gates of Minotauric Logic Plus Another Gate	31
Seven Names of the Minotaur	39
Hacceity without Just Saying It	46
Minoan Cartography	47
Some Things the Minotaur Will Have Said	48
Asterios in other Translations, or: Asterion is the Variation	49

Part Three

Ten Felix Labyrinth Notations	53

Part Four

Ars Minotaurica	71
34° 0' 11" N, 84° 8' 44" W	83
This is Only a Test	93

Acknowledgements	99
Notes	100

PART ONE

Felix with Toolkit

For this experiment, you will need:
projections of other places
disciplines of irony
you will need the Doppler effect
a line-item wrecking crew
one of these, or two
or, three and your dignity
a well-made chair
a taxonomy of beetles
goggles and a scarf trailing behind you
because this happens fast.

For this experiment, you will need
the undeserved trust of scholars
notes scribbled on a peeled apple
or a pair
of apples
you will need declarations of love
lapses in clear thinking
blisters from holding on
a gun at your temple
some clarity on mysteries
a theory of shoes left on the roadside
a left shoe
triumphalism with respect to cake
this photograph of a spruce
more than you can take
all that remains
whomever you think will listen
you will need unhappy secrets
you will need a way out
you will need something to read
to soften
to frame
to jostle
to rebuke
something to condemn

something with waves in it
you will need distortions
and polygons
and unfair assessments
you will need a tongue phantom
an incomprehensible questionnaire
neighbors peering through blinds
you will need cliché
pastorals
invective
compression
hieroglyphics
and, for this experiment, you will need
good intentions
dark suspicions
and the theory of a life lived
in lists
in careful negotiations
in boxes
in Möbius strips
in trouble
in fact
in case
you will need, for this experiment,
everything you lost
each time you forgot
one by one
evasion
convection
you will need to ask for directions
for this experiment
to work
to yield
to transpose
to falter
to fail
You will need it all
and, don't you know,
you will need
a coat.

Dream of the Labyrinth Semiotician

Forget all that nonsense
about unicursal solutions,
multicursal, too; true, you
are lost in amazement
long before you know you're
recursively implicated in
the failed algorithm of
your own construction:
a fractal knot of
survival instincts
educated guessing
careful coordination with the authorities
community outreach
servant leadership
radiating positive vibrations
hand holding
hand wringing
walking-past-the-graveyard-type singing
rethinking your steps
rethinking your life
composing letters to past lovers
confession of transgressions
commission of transgressions
belief in the healing power of laughter
trust in the comforts of comfort food
all that time you wasted pretending to watch Fellini…
none of this will save you.

To be saved is not a Minotauric Art and
is not expressible, down here, as a function
of, say, borders or mereological parts and wholes.
If threads of dark drape over your memory
as planes of rain on glass, that crystalline pane
subsumed in the frame of its limitless closure,
then you see that the existential quantifier
that held your faith and fixed your philosophy
through academic doubt is the inverse operation
and more of a theory of shadow aesthetics
in which the exit Signs will have been,

let's say, controversial and flickering,
weak as fireflies perishing, slow,
fading, a riddle
in a mason jar
in July.

Minotaur's Open Letter to Ovid

Dear O.,

I hate to come on so obvious, but it is I, lurid in the face or phase of your Pasiphaë, a ruined mother, like all others; and that much is true to the history as promulgated in Publius Ovidius Naso, nasal, he knows so, an oblivious no-show. Or am I being churlish?

They (oracles, Sybilline strumpets and doomed mail carriers) claim, but in hushed tones, that your loves are typical triptychs: Amores, domestic advice or private ululations on husbands in absentia, your Heroides, or is it simply that you misplace a poet's sense for the telling detail: poor Medea, Dido, Ariadne, Penelope. Or, to put it more simply: you got your facts wrong. I slice right in-half men who try to sell me on the "comic rule of three."

True there were others who did not look good in the final edits, but sympathetic sun gods and final-act reversals, improbable evasions from Truth are persuasive only in the context of seasonal festivals. Too bad for you, where I come from, the only difference between a Greek Bacchanal and a Roman Saturnalia is the hourly rate for the Eunuchs. And that, baby boy, is not an "issue of translation."

So here it is: paired with Ars Amatoria, The Rape of Sabine Women begins to feels like an equivocation on the act of seduction. It is I, my eye in the face of this recursive burlesque, happy enough to see scholars quibble over the curl of my horns, speculate my casual graffito cleaned up for authorial visits (do you yourself ever come around?), or are we just plain bound to Homeric feet, waiting to be told dread mathematica has finally failed and too-theoretical-for-his-own-good Daedalus retired to Rhodes.

And just when you thought it was safe to read the classics again, Icarus lives on in his foolish, falling, provisional sky.

That's why I look this way and laugh when poets cry.

yours in more ways than one,

M.

Minotaur finds a mirror

Meeting myself was like ghosting some past
beyond the limits of desire in here.
You looked to me as I have looked for light
or its splintered shards pulling me through dark.
I dreamed once that visitors had to sign
in to be recorded as fully dead,
which I confess did seem right at the time,
given all the murderous deepenings
and heroic postulates one might eat;
even my sonnets are incomplete.

In that sense, too, I have been a kind of dreamer,
to dare and wonder if father Minos ever notices the sun.

Pasiphaë with Baby Minotaur
after a 4th century BC kylix

Here, then, are longitudes
of a certain life in parallax
adduced as monster motifs
in the spun worlds of
Etruscan clay.

That we might have been
unloved children of artistic
habituations seems this far on
somehow a churlish and
ungrateful proposition.

It is true enough that
we have had Keats enough
to thank for a vision of the poetic
drama in these arch fabulisms
of encoded space.

                A cut lip to the drinking cup
        is occasion for
        this world to evince

the rupture of its unattended chasms,

                      dread cracking, riven deep into the
        plate tectonics of

consciousness in blood ruin
where is hidden, from
civilized view, the misshapen
dream of our decorative loves,
mutant torpor in dark seams,
all you can ever know
or even finally need
of degenerate beauty suckling close
its sweet and ghastly truth.

Minotauric Equivocations with Shattered Referent Machine

I

We cannot finally discern whether the claim is an imperative "...fix problem: nomenclature" or, rather, merely an indicative: "[the] affix problem is one of nomenclature." We feel like fools asking this, but isn't it just true enough that removing this frightful mask of epistemic modality would make the whole encounter easier to frame, you know, in a seminar setting?

II

On more than one occasion, this felt like a manifestation of our own complicity in the algorithmic view of hide-and-seek games scaled up to mythic enterprise. One argues for the aesthetics of standing around, another the polemical force of turning always left or that it is right to leave turning for those heretically agitating against moving at all, except perpendicular to some putative "given," which we take to mean a punitive "taken."

III

It will have been an editorial decision: plasm[1]
                            Greek[2]
                Labyrinth bone code[3]

[1] the dream of flâneur, Orphic cosmology in certain stochastic streets, unmappbly thus

[2] Euripides in fragmentary love keeps sparse notes; Ovid—Roman, abstruse—won't say which

[3] fissure, fracture, constitutive games or your ludic impostures, deep Lyceum of the splintering horn

```
for (i = 0; i < max; ++i)
    maz[i] = 0;
```

```
    (void) mazegen((x + 1), maz, y, x, rnd);

/ replace the 1's and 0's with appropriate chars */
for (yy = 0; yy < y; ++yy) {
   for (xx = 0; xx < x; ++xx) {
      i = (yy * x) + xx;

      if (yy == 0 || yy == (y - 1))
         maz[i] = hc;
      else if (xx == 0 || xx == (x - 1))
         maz[i] = vc;
      else if (maz[i] == 1)
         maz[i] = fc;
      else if (maz[i - x] != fc && maz[i - 1] == fc
            && (maz[i + x] == 0 || (i % x) == (y - 2)))
         maz[i] = vc;
      else
         maz[i] = hc;      /* for now... */
   }
}
return (0);
```

Five minotauric motivics

nor implaced strictly as light
node clasticity mirrored has
is a principle subsumed by plunge

and go thence from portmanteau
to double integral affect in puppetry
down through as true shadow is

some corner to complementarity of
point to point is intersection of
what will have been born and horns of

these false sweep trysts inside
quintic love or weeping outward
a gravity a material density

turns rigorously into
in two ways in three
lines to which is appended a
line much as dark in modulo

Displacement Theory Song, Sung by Theseus (Unmappably) in a Stochastic Mode

Or, rather, I should say
there are other forms
of imprisonment, that is to say,
of holding one, the Other one
in place, if indeed it is a
place holder for yet other
names and this will have been
as far as I could get without invoking

                how it was that trees
                reconfigured the ambiguous
                moon in its discoverable phases
                as looking up through cracks
                in lives plunged too deeply
                through concentricities of desire

Or, rather, I should say: the lyric reflex, bound thus in chains
                                                      of molecular

revolutions, conceived in the body

                            in some open range of credulity
I wish I had kept   marked by heat and blood
better notes   driven through the syntax of my
head
                            riven with fissures and dislocations
                            the evidence of some spilling fugue

if not just around this corner,
then surely the next.

a point concealed in the vertex of an angle
your angle, I want to say, is perhaps
an architectonic of humility, but my own,
an architecture of stone piles, trace, mark
Or, rather, I should say
that failure is my signature
move in the dark.

Ariadne's Skeptical Daydream

Heroes are fictions, poems lost at sea,
composed in the lurid light
of naïve girlish fantasy,
fabulisms floating on waves of grace.

What traces of me drift
too far from Cretan shores—
pieces of an imagined world
sluicing away to fading maps?

Ironic then that monsters are real
or real enough to hold in thrall
my secret scheme
my deepening dream
of flight from here,
by night, from here
in oracular splendor!
Would that an oracle could see
into the labyrinth of my heart.

doomed as surely
as a victim
in the Minotaur's maze:
a code of corners,
a slow erasure of closing
shadow.

Theseus, slayer of Attic bulls,
sleeps in Athens,
his cosmopolitan Greek sleep,
untroubled by visions
of imprisonment and slaughter.

And should he awake to escape
that halcyon reverie,
what, worth saving,
would remain of me?

L'INFAMÏA DI CRETI
a lyric vernacular

such was the passage down to that ravine.
And at the edge above the cracked abyss,
there lay outstretched the infamy of Crete,
      from The Inferno, Canto XII, Allen Mandelbaum, trans.

I

Even silence conceals a doomed body
and everyone knows the calculation:
strung out along the freeway,
appositives in the trunk, querulous company,
leveraged on miracles and afraid to pull over
not for fear of accusing stares or merciless critique
but for the self-generative jokes we keep in
quantum states until we need them,
exit strategies in metropolitan deliquescence
vignettes shaped on styles probative small talk.

II

Your voice here, a droning whisper in drag,
and none but the most cynical will subtract
from tricks of light these speeches, multiply
nominative in the predicates of sleep
singly true in falsities of travel:
your personal effects marking a trail,
and who knows if you ever find your way back?
horses in bucolic posture; you climb the barbed wire
a covered bridge burned by accident, restored by chance
disclosures draped over you all the while you walk,
as perhaps mythic postulations are somehow
better viewed under the sodium lights of
urban perambulations

III

I was thinking this morning
about the list of things I need
and the list of things I reason
would be among the things I don't
Some things were on the first list
and not on the second while
others were on the second but not the first
And then I started thinking
about what kind of thing would be
on both lists, that is to say:
both things I need
and things I don't.
It seemed to me that this
was somehow more than a
wandering idyll or
an idle wonder or
game played through visions
distant places, in New Mexico,
at night.

IV

I have seen a shattered foot
from the Colossus at Rhodes
and I have smelled perfumes of
of cedars Africana in the North.
And that is a dazzlement
I am scarecly poet enough to write
whether I need to or not,
dreaming of the Fontano Minotauro
water-falling fountain in Taormina, Sicily
or perhaps the appeareance
of the Minotaur in Canto XII
of the Inferno, languid or dying
at the edge of cracked chasm
splayed there for inspection
in the bumbling gloss

V

Creature/Creteure   knowledge in its/their discon-
tents/(dys)contents/Dis
                                    On what scale
Of intimacy does
does the monster arrive in   (simple
undifferentiated brutality,
seminar vestments,
                          which list is invoked to take a roll?

propagators of violence
blasphemers   some-
thing disconcertingly pre-Hellenic)
heretics
those with bad credit history
Ovid's two-formed spectacle
Plutarch's wretched imposture of incurious villainy
Hesiod's stranger textures, his Titans with their primordial preoccu-
pations
Freudian family values
Lacanian abyss

VI

And if the fountain is fluid with stories
washing over stone as through
capillary parodies of blood in your hand
in your head, in the hard fictions of straight lines
etched in unread books, sketches lost among
derelict marginalia of your provable transgressions,
here then is your sculptress, lithe and learned,
it seems, in this light of close study, parlous
perforated in a graphicality of cataclysm
held indeterminately, or else terminally,
on the axis of fluxions in history
inflections across terza rima
schema for un-named investigations
pushed through
the troubled dusts
of secret work.

PART TWO

Seven Gates of Minotauric Logic plus Another Gate

AND

I will keep a diary of this poem
in the open for visitors to inspect:

in its pages they can find a book of absences
and the record of a good idea that abstracted too soon

and I would say that whatever trouble they portend is perhaps
central to the project and, in some way,

the real reason we ever wondered about fugtuive ontologies
and hiding.

OR

Roll me to the rounding of my love
or else modulus 4 at the frontier edge

a place for all the lost balls of a hotel
hallucination to save an ex-girlfriend's

fear of flight and curvature, Alexandria, Carthage, Crete
she climbed the library shelf and fell toward Minoan sex in specific gravity

Or else I was there in sleep, in accelerations, and inflected light.

NOT (A LAB) NOT (A LABYRI)*)

Not a rave review, I think
Not a rare appearance, I hope

Not a trace of usable evidence, I suspect
Not a one like it to be found around here

Not a good start to this
Not a bad ending after all

Not if I have anything do with it.

* nth

X(OR)

It is not the case that we have so many
who would build the maze machine

without first considering what
it will do to the other machines

there are systems of equations and protocols
you may remember from a contextual time

so, whatever eats must fail, must fail fully

X(NAND)

The problem of addition is one of fiction
the way a fantasy is propagated across

the missing parts of speech, or that every is each
an essential piece, which arrives a month later,

exotic in the packaging, odd to the touch
and terrible in its finality:

Theseus, without reliable tools, will have gone down into cold and dark.

N(AND)

You write about the sound,
for so few will ever get to hear it

you wonder if the most important detail
is maybe the part you cannot hear: the subsonic, the turgid whisper,

and you scribble for hours; this is hardest part:
the thing shows or it doesn't and then:

I mean to say but cannot: that closure is some sound we will have known.

N(OR)

There is an old truck at the intersection of
Sunset and Santa Monica Boulevard

painted the colors of this great country:
Red, White and Blue and with no ironic distance

I will sleep in that truck tonight, eating an egg sandwich I stole from
my porn-shop job*
listening to hustlers tripping by, sucking toward some rueful dawn,
edge of allegiance

waiting, not to say, wishing for someone to ask me what it will have
been.
(I searched for Greek monstrations in the blown-out lots of memory.)

* The owner was a crystal-meth fiend. His mother had sent egg-salad and fried-egg sandwiches, which he never ate and which I took, not without shame, from his basement desk before they rotted on pens and needles. He collected jars of mayonnaise and fired me summarily for drawing pictures of Medea slaughtering her children, after the 19th colorist, Eugène Delacroix. I drew this picture on a legal pad, but that hardly makes any of it legal: I swept floors and heard a woman scream. A customer claimed to have made his fortune selling bowties to pig-boys. My Minotauric strategy is to go back and work there, to map a space for the empty day. I made like the Hellenic in my best escape, off stage, under cover night, which was, after all, day inside Not (Day) or After.

X(NOR)

No one even really understands this; it is complex
and one finds many disagreements on fine points

Indeed, it is as if the theory outstrips itself,
and that seems comic enough to a fool like me

but what if something goes seriously wrong?
what if we simply cannot understand the problem?

Oidoi singers sing songs about epic preparations

Seven names of the Minotaur

BAAL-MOLOCH

Put your history behind doors
and imagine the Greek without

translations to place and systems
of space and pleasure in things hidden.

Here are only witnesses to dreams
or seminars and pictures in books

as one might love to know are known.

TALOS

I am thinking now of conflicting
accounts in the collective inquiry

of certain scholars who presume
to reclaim our truth before

veils of history are draped over
with texts of sleepwalking madmen.

I cannot remember my own name.

SHEDU

Suppose the family is not your
name but your heart or your face,

and however the night converges
on your love, there is yet some

possibility for this language,
inside out, under the bed, through your eyes,

and this is more than they will want you to see.

APIS

The rattling of keys on a chain
has frightened the cats again

and Aegyptians will tell you
when the sky is yet open

enough to taste the irony
in the way you read this line

and in the manner you leave me here.

USHI-ONI

It is a box and not some other
as you may have wondered

as you are surely expected to ask
as who would not think to suppose

as to the contents therein
as far as can be discerned

a box a box thus the thing it is.

ASTERION

I consulted three versions of this
and found each a fabulism of

eponymic flourishes but not at all
inconsistent with a fractured view

of the trajectory of Western voice
speaking over itself in reflexive jests,

having not finished a sentence in four thousand years

PRODIGIUM

Keep your secrets behind a door
and permit only those who

can do the most damage to
your memory to inspect the evidence,

your repertory of
improperly annotated worlds

filled with words you did not write.

Haccheity without just saying it

Which of us had it:
those unfinished and broken
structures appear
lovely
in lateness(?)

I didn't write any of it
down,
          as I should, you know,
because I am responsible
for what will have been said here.
I think they agreed in principle
to give me a certain interpretive latitude
when, in all truth, some longitude
might finally have proved
the greater gesture

Minoan cartography

There is a game to be adduced here,
and I can confess somewhat to feeling--
as I trace the arcs of a life
through your clean rooms or
along my unmappable streets
across the colonnades of false triumphs
with their tattered bunting stinging the wind—
that this sequence of play, if indeed it ever ends,
will not end well.

The penitent topologist knows the numbers are
arranged against him and his pretension to knowledge,
but to unroll these charts is to find love in fractal fossils
and perhaps to recover some dignity
in marching off forever
in the wrong direction
dropping bread crumbs
down the through the reductio.

Just add absurdum.

And that's the kind of cheap jest for which I must be punished,
    for permitting this to go on.
Anyway, it sounds like prose by now.

Only that the word was good enough
to begin with but irretrievably corrupt by
the time we made it to the border
And I can admit a certain perverse (but informed) thrill in leaving
behind those provincials and their quaint notions of spatial relationships
In any case, the first one to the frontier
gets to lick the door and kiss the witch,
just like coming home.

Some things the Minotaur will have said

Know two ways about it

Write to the edge of shadow

Place it before you

It is implaced

Surgery was a solution

Someone should rethink the schematics

Push as one pushes pull to be push

A further a letter a

Sing as what would be sung in dark places

Someone moved ninety degrees and was cornered

Plural terms will get you nowhere good(s)

A tessurae

An imbrication

A lurid stare from a logical positivist

Place it behind you

A plunder a mediation

Querulous petitions

Around it goes

A round object shows

America

America

A mirror cut

Pray in the morning heat and (same) which to gather is be

Asterios in Other Translations, or: Asterion is the Variation

the graphical
        or better perhaps to say
      magical paper
here folded into certain provocative
shapes
is the first evidence I present in
my theory-of-the-world-as-labyrinth
                        you
know these kinds of projects are begun
and almost never

                completed

and this, too, is part of the aesthetic claim:
that some pathways lead to yet others
while some go no   where   at
                all

whatever else is true of the paper,
                its center,
                its putative margins

one should not expect clarity, resolution, and certainly no
illumination
it is dark in here and impossible to read
the map
I want to think
        here about
I seem to recall
having once wondered
whether criticism must
                follow the art, causally,
                which is to say: in the causal chain

First the objet d'art, then the critical condition
or as an act to be imagined,
vulnerable in empty rooms
if I peel away the trust from my hands
knotted in exegetical semaphore

touch this place   motion to go

put the art

before the course
so, too, with matters of
lost to the ravages of
in a world of
you will have
          known

PART THREE

Ten felix labyrinth notations

I

Felix, you are here.
This is where
we will have found you,
hiding in the evidence room
with fiends and clowns,
desperate to give consent,
mad to drink whatever is milk
to the confidence men
in their coterie of roped
villains, rubrics to the
grave, entrenched at the border.

II

I don't think you have any idea
what we have been through,
what we endure just to get your attention
these days; it's almost as if you have given up
on the schematics, all those auditions,
to say nothing of the space itself:
capacious as a rift in something like love.
Begin with a simple motive,
curled and dense
with economies of discarded syllables
and surface tensions in the ruin.
This is where you are, Felix.

III

And if you can believe the reports
there are preoccupations to fear
inherited traditions and invocations.
From the cedar tree, you see purple
arcs the evening clouds; none of this new
none of this is according to
and which is a sure sign of
breaking inside the crafts
of waking before a refulgent sky
a weak seam in the tree's trunk
folding you downward
into the soil, compositions of
undifferentiated clay
riven with stars or rivulets
if that is what you find
will bring the two together,
in the magnetic vistas,
and consensual imprisonments
you call outward.

IV

GRAMM(ARIA)

If I read you
you will have been something
oracular in my books,
a node of known things,
held out to final analysis,
held over for another week.

If I read you
you are perhaps to have understood
or it is the color of my looks
a code of what showing means
spelled out in my marginalia
spelled slowly to keep the tones.

Because I read you today
you are reading me here,
as one might imagine the lines
graphed too closely, peeled from
their numerical pulps,
consigned to notes of the foot,
how I fell through a swarm of
semicolons, readerly affectations
of le page de deux
and ink on the verso.

Now that I am reading you
and after you are thus read
I will have felt a new cut
riven through this discourse
we have made on chains of
desire and open clotures of
dim philosophy,
how I climbed through
the sound of your alarums
torwad a periodcity
but no period, no suspensions
in the verdict, no vertex in
the sentence.

Let me read you and, having been
a reader thus, I will have myself
been read or, let me mark this page
with rules and constitutive games,
with paints and gramarye
with some modicum
of my reckless trust
that the book is written out
that the book goes on
that the book is our shelter
in the modal tense,
that the book will have been
what we needed
to be.

V

CHATTAHOOCHEE ONTOLOGY

This, then, is as my head is
uncoiled in some reduplicative frame
some obscure obscene name given to
rivers flowing backward to their tributaries,
fragments of dimming history
glimpsed through holes in the proof.

You are my eye in parallax, fixed to
the departing view, of that which will have been
immovable and held between shifting states,
reagent chains in unwritten worlds,
encoded somehow in the syntax
of your laughter, which is or is not
as your hands are
sharp, by your own admission
and drawn upward in droll vignettes
of caution or warning or embrace,
to correct for the splintered light,
for the familiar drift
toward magic
and noumenal improvisations.

This, then, is as my memory is
swept through auricles,
through chambers,
backward to radical concealments
and dreams of touch.

VI

CRETAN FIELD WORK

                I am concerned here to say something cogent about *
                we are having with the marginalia, indeed with
the   margins
We do not trust these wild experimentalists as they appear, at best, irresponsible
and, at worst, morally transgressive

*(the problem)

...clearly not what I meant by that although I cannot say now just what it was
Whom do you think would follow these clinamen as if lost to sudden walls
as if proved or loved in the given trace, where moonglow dimples the spiders' webs
with fissures of secret light
Give us the dread motifs of naturalism's false vision
I give you fig trees and their milky sacks, plump with burgeoning mysteries
of seed and soil and triage to the tongue in backyards, in baseball.
...or could have simply eaten the pear if indeed that's what it
...not, in the last analysis ** to solve or resolve or to even to contemplate
as philosophy, even the marginal, presumes to do, as it is known to become a work

**(my problem)
We liked speaking this way
when complexity made us feel free
and history would not move beyond
the chairs in our front room

Hark, what late theory songs
reduced to deepening folds of
evanescence and forgetting
that the past is perhaps for getting

and bringing to fallen porch swings
and these parodies of determinism.

I will have walked toward these margins
and made *** of what I could see,
structural representations of the rest,
of my own rest if I belong to the
page after this is written,
if they let me stay
if I remain

                                  ***(drawings, but I'll call them maps)

VII

FELIX, LOST WITH TWO FALSE SAINTS, AND A HAINT

Your home is built with fragments
on a substrate of analeptic dolls
emissaries, one supposes, from the older
way of doing things

You have said that tradition would require
systems of rain and oracles and then, just as quickly,
no more, please.

Take your habituations of counting and methodologies
and pray for decent weather,
decent food,
decent rumors, at least.

Let that cracking tableau be the harbinger of Saint Doubles,
my new trajectory, the final face on my vapor trail of desire,
It is as one and two will have been the numbers of the eaten,
the structure of a geometricity, a system this time of thunder storms.

And who among us will not have felt a certain urgency about the sky
in its duplicitous arrangements with chicken little,
head cut clear off, pursued through liturgical imposture
by Saint Lucent in his neo-logistic idiom:
faces in the vesper trails, ministerial, accusatory, inconsolable,
impenetrable, full of love.

Clarity, then, is the mission here, the daily devotional
of clean visio and Aquinas in the color field.
Everyone in attendance will recall the lessons moving
toward claims of proportio and integritas
and how lucid language spilled out from under the diva's
gossamer ball gown in a parthenogenetic flood of good will.

And still, there were those who found, who find, it all
just mysterious enough to accept without all the unsettling tropes of
responsible inquiry; let's call it a question
of decorum over
bad form,
leaning on the walls of Labyrinths.

Double, however, remains twice the name if you see the saint,
if you say your reveries are innocent and clearly divided against
known quantities, known associations; do not further imagine that
Lucent is else or that one is madness or two is too simply written
as one or some other plus the flood water, plus the visio, plus the sky.
All you wanted was the house, maybe, then too, some stories about a
country witch.
And that is a canvas of erasure
that will have been
erased.

VIII

FELIX'S QUADRATIC LOVE STORY

Blockhead thinks of factorials
or dreams of a theoretical prime;
he understands nothing,
is mortal and stupid
and writes like this.

Bubbles sends a letter
or supposes the number line
a ghost in composite shades
gathered in toward an equation
one should write in this way.

Look at Blockhead in the gallery
and imagine he has a vision
of some distant metropolis,
suspended in the liquid alphabet
of confession, of flight.

Look, then, at Bubbles at her work
fingers, slender and deliberative
in the slopes of cause
or curve of effect
in planetary arcs, in arboreal parks.

Blockead either does or does not know
that Bubbles is his own faith
in the problem, not of time but memory
itself folded as linen with the edges parallel
as from the streets outward
or never exactly home.

Bubbles either will or will not keep
such patterns as one might believe
the truth in some square-skull
philosophy to be imputed values, bottom to top
fissures in the cranium, cracked
to make room for anything that might grow.

IX

FELIX IN THE GIVEN WORLD

I read somewhere that no one knows
the age of the planet, our planet,
that estimates are theoretical doggerel
and range from 4.5 billion years to
just this morning, after we woke but
before you noticed something odd
in the color of the autumn sun.

In the dream you wondered aloud, why
as a matter of style, that I sometimes
repeat myself, why I say things twice,
and not only that, but also why
other times, I do not?

Your objection, I understood, turned
on the question of intent and perhaps
also content, if that makes any sense.
And even if it does not,
that is how it was.

Will you believe my true story of
whirling and swooping on a tire swing
and feeling as though I were clinging to
the pendulum of an absurdly large clock?
I wandered the earth on certain promises
negotiated, in absentia, with my memory,
improvisatory histories I suppose
(in any case, that's how I will explain them)
touching the light, filaments of gray in my hair
touching the night.

As a boy, I wanted to be an intellectual.
Now, I am happy to be considered agreeable
and fit for good company.
This is central to my theory of the world,
my epistemological vision in which a
name is known as the man is seen or where
the rocks are held because they are heavy

to the palm and compel us outward on
the appositives of our convictions, our faith.

It is not true that I went back
to that tire swing years later and found
the pendulum chain had grown into the tree,
not true that I tried to wrest that chain
from the unjust grasp
of a past that was, in any event
never mine.

Never mind anything I say,
but I am struggling to quantify
the age of these toys I found in my
parents' attic: billions of years I suspect.
I believe in causation and thunder
and also the aleatoric effects of laughter
without provocation. This is only one
of my naïve sentiments, and I wish
I had the time and courage
to defend my position.

But I can agree with you that the sun
this morning did indeed
seem oddly tilted, strangely translucent
draping our ancient and new-born selves
in its healing quilt, and
I wanted to kiss your hand
I wanted to kiss your hand

X

MODAL MAPS AND TROPES ENOUGH TO HANG ONESELF WITH

This way to the openings
and that way, perhaps, to something
other than the properly folded space
of memory, of a maze.

Light has a scattered and lost look
diffracted around the corners of your story
older than the properties of a molded face
of symmetry, of a haze.

Here, then, is a vision of multicursal and controversial
solutions, fractals if anyone remembers those, some rhizomic
cartography
               of your heart

PART FOUR

Ars Minotaurica

Set into this sun the city street
down from known names
up through thrown pleasures
that it will have been a day for writing
is certain to tremulous hands,
knots in the thread,
not one's own
looping into recombinant love,
the tongue the twist the trysting players
lost in nomenclatures
thus are written dark revisions
as propagations of forgetting
as memory will have been,
in costume, derelict gods
A penitential voice
is somehow the given term
inscribed on those querulous faces
waiting for summer,
a spine on the sky,
honey and hair,
inlumino Creti

Here will have been a rubric song of representations in winds, a Corus antecedent for Subsolanus.

St. Theseus in his numinous and fictive fold sings:

...not from contested shore nor else the stone blare of Afer ventus or Vulturnus under happy sail to you , to mistress Agean...

Say it:

hacceity

one of seven systems (One (sing)ular)

the spine, the spline; One shipbuilder, One arc under Earth's sphere

Perabsurdus:

as performance is a forgery
is a phantasmic plasm,
does not happen,
will not have occurred,
not in a mirror,   ply between if across is
never in space,
clever modulations   no future for false quantities
modalities in fact of   as, rather, One or as
monstration in the light   Another in vague
of dim, dripping lamps   quodlibets of Two

frames out of the page
You cannot find it here
Here is doggerel   in rivers, too
is architecture   or as St. Minos in reversal
is problematica   of some revenance, an epistolary disjunctive
is conjugation of motifs   of sudden memory, fading light
incurvatus in se
so they say
in the providential secrecy
of rooms where dialogue is held
where is made verso
where is spelled recto   what vision will have made
where is skin torso   of Piacasso a missing saint,
in the book   revenant of the canvas

Perabsurdus to St. Minos

Translate the world to split the codex
and keep yourself a little bauble of counterfactuals
surprised to find this vision
we cannot all pretend to be the other person
someone kept a diary.
another kept a close watch.
and it was seen.
gates or doors
it was known to have been this way
and not that

> This will have been the site of a certain cogenda
>
> St. Theseus sings:
>
> ...this will have been an act of colligenda in the guise of grace or
>
> How it is held
>
> provably
>
> from transgression
>
> to things of a truth

I will know this place by the evidence it keeps.
You will see your face through questions it does not ask.
She can find my trace in the puzzles I would not solve.
He can leave someplace and hide in the other space.
It is not the proper moment to run from the room.
We are never wrong about the hopes we fail.
You may fail enough to learn what sleep conceals.
They have come to show us how it happens.
I will leave puzzles through your wrong room.
You can solve the hopes if your sleep will leave.
She will know to have other evidence for show.
He would not ask to keep your proper questions.
It happens someplace that the trace obviates the moment.
We do not hide hopes in the evidence.
You will never fail to run.
They will conceal the other face.

This "un-named source," if it is one,
might appear to you his street clothes
and maybe he too is being watched
or maybe it is an appointment,
something to be kept as one keeps:
keeps the faith
keeps the secret
keeps the comatose on certain drugs

And if a source is a material,
then you are left with blueprints
spread out, encoded as fabric
on the hood of your truck
or mine
or maybe you have a picture
in your head in which the shape
of a hand move across your hand
the angles of the shade are all wrong
the courtroom transcript is garbled
someone else was there
or maybe it is none of my business
to whom these monologues are addressed
and in that case the rule has not changed:
keep talking.

Here is a name, a sounded-out player
in whatever vignette you are proposing here:
the princess, if she is one, is locked in the library
the princess, if she will admit her faults, is to
blame
your so-called source is a mole, not a counter-spy,
but an actual mole, digging in your garden
and establishing some basic assumptions

Or maybe, you have been on holiday
and are shocked to discover the dishes
were interlocking pieces of some vast, ceramic
mobile

Or maybe you only think you are an artist who can keep:
keep a routine
keep the change
keep it to yourself

> And you could simply pretend you never considered any of this; it is your word against whomever you find here
> Or maybe plausible deniability is what we have always wanted for each other but never for ourselves and something we keep:
> keep going
> keep coming back
> keep still

Here, then, was one house
pencil sketched at one remove,
from hallway dust to mirror
silver in certain dim
modulations of trust

if that's what we want it to be,
wish it, thereby, to have been

There are your books of field work,
the watercolors that washed through
afternoon fogs, retreats, odd music.
Here are the water towers that
broke my theoretical heart exactly along
the fault lines.

And this was no simple truth,
was no truth at all, really: held together
with plaster, candle wax, or
shoe strings tangled in some
fervent investigation of
the hallway
the dust,
the mirror
the screened porch with
the hydrangea just outside

As from a true sky, it is made

in the garding memory
of home
the grinding bowl
in sympathetic powders,
elixirs of faith
tincture of holding and what is held
to be the case, to be sure, in place
as it is folded back into
your specific gravity
your knowing return
from this,
unmappably thus

Felix wants to believe in the prophetic properties
of certain visions he's been having, like the one
just this morning in which a version of himself,
he supposes, approaches a wall (or is it a canvas?
a page?) and writes:

"All Felix's endings are happy ones."

To be sure, this will have some odd resonance on the street
where our man is somewhat known as a purveyor of grim
portents
and decidedly not known for speaking plainly
or even comprehensibly about the given world.

He considers his dreamed words as one might
search for a curve in the evidence of a straight line,
or as so many have imagined reveries to conceal
important truths, relations that dramatize their own falsi-
ties.

This is precisely the kind of portentous moment he has
tried to write before or, in any case, the kind he has tried,
with mixed success, to write about.

And it is the impulse to sort out that distinction
that moves Felix's eyes to the pattern of veins
running through his hands,
the texture of his skin,
a vague shadow somewhere overhead,
his endings,
his paint,
his pen.

Will you be in my opera?

You are the logic of my soliloquy, my sonnet.
And I have here some new lines to free the old
from their strange commitments, their loosely strung promises.

When Charles Bukowski died,
I was anchored to a zero-sum game theory,
a predicate of misdirected loves,
an inventory of unclaimed modalities
sluicing away to foreign shores,
to opposite numbers,
to a voice behind the shades in a house two streets over
but with no address
in my Los Angeles concomitant;
the hour was late, the opera indeterminate.

Do you believe that I have written this before?
I suppose, then, it is left for me
to open my papers to the revisions
of a time when you were not among my correspondents,
when I was Genesee or North Martel
or, yes, even the Madman Manqué of Hollywood Proper.

True, it was ever without you
or a priori,
but I improvised songs

with Alabama thematics,
and I saw a Rose Window
in a downtown church.

All the talk of an empty

space

seemed to us not only fanciful
but probably seditious.
Our own paradoxes were
humiliation enough,
and, indeed we imagined

                                      chorus lines of
                                      phantom logicians
                                      streaming through

half-

(opened doors.)

This was neither exactly
the lost memory of
some silent apparition
haunting the corridors
nor the explicit regret of

                                      having forgotten your face
                                      because, of course, we kept
                                      you close
                                      even as we watched

you vanish
into the recombinant
mosaic of others'
puzzled lives and
contingent worlds.

In the end, however,
our only true delight was
in believing you were
never gone
but only crossing,
anew,
your known
frontier.

You were never as much
the whispered construction
of my twilit story as when I,
a man of no dazzlements,
kissed through mist your
nocturne,
your vesperial similitudes
- not lips from fantasy
or prophetic rumination
or even deeply circulating
rumor -
but your inversions
of sky and ground,
your projections of keeping,
your mosaics of magnolia
where
our roots converged, entangled,
and pushed upward from
purple
toward the provisional moon.

Here it is.
And you are still there to see
how the final analysis will
read until such fixities as remain are
better understood

Whistling is another of your glib
assertions to the contrariety, or
have I misrepresented the good work
you were claiming to have done
with subcontractors and subways
and subalterns?

True enough, I recall having said,
that history is annunciative in its
most delicate moments and
obscurantist at the margins,
which is another way of suggesting
that daily myth is an economy of scale:
too big to be merely false

Felix is having some second thoughts about the way this prose poem looks, not so much about how it reads, to say nothing of what it might all add up to, but its aspect is problematical. Indeed, its aspect ratio is altogether contrary to what he wanted to accomplish here, which was something else troubled him, finding a project, finding the right project: an open letter to career solipsists; a thought experiment in which contemporary "types" become the creatures in a kind of post-modern bestiary (should he include The Mother? The Last Woman?), and a defense of verse (not this one) written in bed.

For all these projects, Felix is deploying his new alterity machine, his puppet Other. He is doing this to test the claim that some others are Oneself, which is to say: one's Self. At the same time, it amuses him to name him "False Felix," probably hoping to invoke the False Florimell from The Faerie Queene or, somehow perhaps, to suggest that he has read and understood all of Paul Ricoeur's Oneself As Another. In fact, he has not.

Of course, the difficulty on all these counts begins when he reminds us that this very prose-poem is of uncertain authorship, was conceivably written by, is possibly being written by that same False Felix. Descartes, in despair over his daughter's death, is said to have commissioned, in the likeness of his daughter, a working automaton, which he kept in his home and which he loved.

Perhaps then, what Felix has here, despite his attempts to ruin everything with speculative self-reflexivity, is the working likeness of a prose-poem or, in any event, the puppet Other of one, struggling in unfamiliar company to say the correct lines, to laugh at the appropriate moments, to figure out how loves feels, what the sky wants, whom to believe, whom to doubt, and, when waking, how to look surprised.

I want to believe you are the Self
that I have imagined I should be.
And I know that the names of things
are not the same as the things they name.

So, I am wondering if you wouldn't mind
going out into the world for me today, that is,
going as me, in my place,
moving through my spatial coordinates,
eating what is mine, spilling through my face.
I am interested in knowing
what is going on out there:
how it happened,
what is being said
and what is being done about it.

I saw you standing in the hall last night,
looking at yourself,
myself in the mirror,
and it occurred to me that some recourse
to the philosophy of mirrors
might be instructive here:
they tell us very little
as they are vast, even infinite fictions,
and are epistemologically, you know,
inconclusive.

.

Last night I saw something unfamiliar in the mirror.
And I wonder if you might consider this sweet fraudulence:

Look at me, Minotaur.
Now, look away.

34° 0' 11" N, 84° 8' 44" W
N34 0.17189 W84 8.6796
*coordinates of Duluth, GA by degrees, minutes, seconds
and by GPS decimal minutes*

One could say there exists
no language for this
kind of speculative enterprise,
summoned from signs,
portents, vagaries, vapor trails.

One might suggest a skyline in view
or if only, then also merely
the consolations of sky.

Or here, then, if you insist
is the characteristic move
of the skeptic in some domestic guise,
draped, as ever, in flummery
escaping out on lost county roads,
the classic style of villainy in flight.

"There were very few clouds that evening and it was still
light enough for me to see for many miles,"

"The[y] continued to watch it and it was soon lost from sight
in the darkness and clouds."

"It moved slowly across the sky, along and above a nearby
tree line, and eventually vanished
from sight."

~ from the records of MUFONGA,
Mutual UFO Network of Georgia.

THREE CARTOGRAPHIC GESTURES

1871

Congressman J. Proctor Knott of Kentucky delivers, on the floor of the U.S. House of Representatives, a satirical speech "On the Untold Delights of Duluth," pursuant to debate over a railroad subsidy connecting two major commercial points in Wisconsin but passing through the small, inconsequential(?), Duluth. His observations are amusing, pointed, and occasionally Parminedean: "But the fact is, sir, Duluth is pre-eminently a central place, for I am told by gentlemen who have been so reckless of their own personal safety as to venture away into those awful regions where Duluth is supposed to be, that it is so exactly in the centre of the visible universe that the sky comes down at precisely the same distance all around it."

Late 6th, early 5th Century BCE

Poet-philosopher Xenophanes speculates on the nature of the universe and, in Aëtius's fragments, seems to posit an "upper limit of earth" visible from the ground and through which he (Xenophanes) imagines his stylized meteorology. He declares the moon a compressed cloud. That his writings occupy a liminal space between whimsical scientificity and lyrical inquiry seems to me another way of calculating the location of interiorities.

1686

Gottfried Wilhelm Leibniz formulates his principle of the Identity of Indicernibles, an ontological axiom that says

$\forall F(Fx \leftrightarrow Fy) \rightarrow x=y$ If two objects share exactly the same properties, then they are identical, from which is derivable,

$x = y \rightarrow (\forall F)(Fx \leftrightarrow Fy)$ If two object are identical, then they share all the same properties, sometimes called the principle of the Indiscernability of Identicals.

The principles seem to call themselves into question, which may be their greatest insight. We might want to wonder how far these conditions extend and whether things must both be what they are and where they are? Certainly Leibniz himself anticipates a range of problems and objections, but obvious—and, by now, intuitive—

grammatological and quantum-mechanical speculations permit suggestive, if not decisive, critiques.

THREE KNOTS

Probability

I received in the mail today my crazy check
which reminds me of all my mistakes
and places me in good company, I think,
peering through a sheet of paper
and seeing in its brutal grain
the evidence of what went wrong

and so much lost time in the dotted line

Flemish Eight

You would be limitless
and I would be theoretical
over the principles in hollow
space spelled out, drawn through
a crescent of shadow, film, fiddle
and summary judgments

pulled away from plural, from plenum

Eye Splice

A see of visio
Aquinas in parallax
some objects in mirror appear
stranger than they are
others will perhaps have been
a sea, a proviso, a double-refracted flood

                    blinds open

*

I am in bed, paging through a graphic novel and expecting the worst,
almost forgetting to look up and scan the television for evidence
of an expressive motif for this moment.
Instead, I see there another Fassbinder film:

Welt am Draht
Querelle
Berlin Alexanderplatz

I don't understand anything.
His self-conscious deployment
of the camera reminds me
that film-makers ask us,
in the lover's desperate tone,
to read their hearts at twenty-four frames per second,
falling from the roof at 9.8 meters per second
to push through
the rejected scripts
of a life cut
to running times
spheric derivations
for a cruelty of the page.
And don't you agree that it is
precisely that grasping
toward humility's ruin
that becomes, in any narrative,
in this story,
the final emblem
of credulity.

Die bitteren Tränen der Petra von Kant
Angst essen Seele auf,
In einem Jahr mit 13 Monden

I know what it means.
But I do not
understand
what it wants.

It was something Ed said.
And I think too it was
the way Ed said it,
the way Ed is known to say
certain things, which others have said
only Ed can, in that way, say.
I want to say this and also to say
it's time perhaps that we
started listening to Ed, that is,
to what Ed says,
to what Ed is saying.

Some will say he says "this" and others
may claim he says "that." And rightly so.
Ed says so much it's hard to keep from noticing
Ed is never not saying something.
Indeed, it would be more correct to say:
Ed is always saying something to the extent
that it might more remarkable than not
to find a moment when Ed says nothing.
Which is to say: if there is anything
to be said about it, Ed will say it
or, more fantastically, that Ed has said it.

Ed, Ed, Ed, Ed,
Ed, Ed, Ed.   *The Eastern Continental Divide is said to*
I hear you,   *run under the Old City Hall.*
and I think I know   *Ed does not, however, claim to know.*
what you're trying to tell me.
I think I know
what you're trying to tell us.
What do you say, Ed?
What about it?
What's going on here, Ed?
What should we do?

Ed says keep up the good work.
Ed says nod to neighbors.
Ed says live with some risk.
Ed says it's all in the wrist.
Ed says 'you be the judge.'
Ed says empty sets are full of projects.
Ed says go some way.

Ed says something every day.
If Ed says it, then I'll take his word for it:
Ed's word.
The word of Ed.

Ed is not a horse.
That was a different problem.
Ed is not an alter ego.
He lives in Duluth.   ←
Ed is not an experiment.
Ed is not a strategy.
Ed is not a point of departure,
or a misunderstanding, or a special interest.
Though it is true Ed speaks in a recognizable way,
Ed is not a "way of speaking."
Ed himself admits this could get complicated.

Ed does not have representation.
Ed knows how to wait patiently.
Ed is not what you would call "results oriented."
Ed says he is happily out of the loop.

Let's say Ed runs a race and loses:
Ed will be the first to congratulate the winner

Suppose Ed accidentally kills a stranger:
Ed will tearfully turn himself in
to the authorities and, in so do doing,
turn himself into the authorities.

Do you see the difference?

Ed says you should cultivate some humility.
Ed is up-front about his intentions.
Ed declares his delight.
Ed asserts surprising truths.
Ed avers that life has been good.
Ed says things could be worse.
Ed says the cake is delicious.
Ed says this while vacationing in Crete.
Say, Say, Say, Say
Say, Say, Say

That is how I heard him.
And others will affirm
my view with perhaps
this one proviso:

Ed is the voice
in which we say
our names
our pleasures
our institutions
our sleep-talking drollery.

So think of me if it helps,
but don't quote me.
Tell them Ed said so.

"An adult resident of N.E. metro Atlanta observed a bright star-like light toward the west of which she took photos. The light moved down and went off like an electric light, then came back on. Venus or other celestial bodies may be responsible here depending on which way the witness was really looking."

"Each acceleration was accompanied by electric-like trails."

"The witness would not respond to e-mail or telephone calls."

> ----*from the records of MUFONGA,*
> *Mutual UFO Network of Georgia.*

Herr Fassbinder,

In a 1954 article, for The Journal of Philosophy, B.A.G. Fuller observes that the "recent sightings of so-called, 'Flying Saucers,' whatever their origin, should remind [us] that man's belief in his central, unique, and privileged metaphysical status in the universe may be mistaken…" This seems like a reasonable provocation, and I wonder if you can imagine a films scenario in which the question of alien morality is played out during a passage by train from Frankfurt to Bucharest. The traveler is the foreigner on holiday from a distant point of light. He is dressed as a woman and carries a Polish passport. His luggage is Italian, his hat blocked in a London haberdashery. If he remains in Europe, he risks infecting the planet with a pathogen quite harmless on his world, but certain death for humans. If, however, he leaves before his scheduled return, he will die of despair.

Stockholm to Rome.

Sarajevo to Marseilles.

Rennes to Warsaw.

Warsaw to Łódź.

He notes in his travel diary the striking images
in an illuminated Haggadah,
painted by Arthur Szyk, born 1894, Łódź,
died 1957, New Canaan, Connecticut.

The Seder Plate.
The Four Questions.
The Bread of Affliction

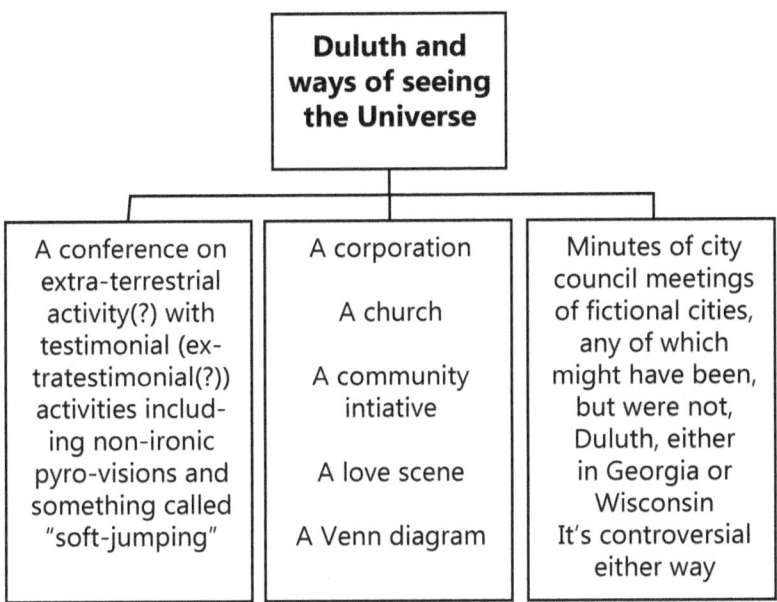

Dear Ed of Duluth, Georgia

You know how the sky bends toward color in late afternoon.

You know what will work here and what will fail.

You know the area codes for all of Wisconsin are 715, 262, 414, 908, 608, and 920.

You know, too, that 920 is an overlay area code for 414, so let's not go too far in that direction.

I know you understand what we're saying, Ed. And I really do sense we have made progress. This reminds me of the time we ran screaming down Magnolia Avenue, somewhere in Alabama.

You know that was summer.

A long time ago.

Herr Fassbinder,

It is 1995 and I am climbing into an attic in Los Angles. There among the detritus of many generations' inhabitants is the fragment of a program note for a Saturday salon held in the home of George Balanchine, who lived briefly on North Fairfax in Hollywood. For reasons not entirely unrelated to this moment, I am thinking often of Stravinsky and am pleased to imagine him at one of these weekend affairs. Of course, I know Balanchine and Stravinsky had a long, important artistic relationship as composer and choreographer; in 1938 certainly, and perhaps also at other times, both lived on the Hollywood/West Hollywood axis. Stravinsky is the Russian-French émigré and Balanchine from Georgia, the far edge of Europa.

Now, my host explains to me that the attic and part of the living room below us are all that remains of the house as it was when rented briefly in 1949 or 1950 by Anäis Nin. I confess all this appears specious at best and spurious at least, but don't you know that Vera Zorina, Balanchine's former wife, performed in Arthur Honneger's Joan of Arc at the Stake at the Hollywood Bowl in the August of 1949. Both Stravinsky and Zorina's former husband, Balanchine himself, were in the audience.

In my mind, I cannot resist linking Anäis Nin to the bizarre androgyny of Jean d'Arc, somehow through the geometry of Stravinsky's Apollon Musagète, choreographed, of course, by Balanchine. There are four roles in that work: Apollo, Terspichore, Polyhymnia, and Calliope, three muses.

It is 1995 and I live near Balanchine's old address:

North Fairfax Avenue to its dead-end

on Hollywood Boulevard,

look both ways,

take a right.

This is Only a Test

Critics have contended that the machine [the CERN Hadron Particle Accelerator] could produce a black hole that could eat the Earth or something equally catastrophic. ~ New York Times

Let me see if I understand this:
Just outside Geneva, in a land of neutral zones,
scientists and pretenders to science are
contemplating a particle collision experiment
that some believe could open a black hole and end the world:
cascading protons, shot in opposite directions
at ninety-nine percent of the speed of light
around a giant, underground, internationally-funded loop
                                        of human desire.

So, certain things are infinite, I suppose, and others last
what, a trillionth of a second(?), the length of time
they are measuring in Switzerland, staging that instant
                                        after the Big Bang.
And it turns out that part of the machine is actually in France,
which gives me hope.

The truth is I want to trust the romance of a visionary madness,
to look past the apocalyptic overtones—because that's what I do--
                                        and toward
a myth, a dream of revelation, a quantum state of insight.

To prepare for this, I might recall Icarus plummeting from
some unimaginable height, his wings melted not so much
by the heat of Phoebus's flaming chariot as, rather,
by the light of close scrutiny, of observable facts,
or by the received view that humans should not fly.

Perhaps it is a consolation to find, in all those black-and-white
                                        film clips
of absurdly improbable, planes flapping, gyrating, churning,
                                        twirling, some

argument for the failure of any rational enterprise.

And one could do worse than to end up in a Breugel painting,
each day, dressing up for the same lyrical end, replaying,
repeating,
returning round again, to the limits of philosophy
                                          and Flemmish high culture,
that moment when it all went wrong.

Like so much else, the Hadron Collider's properly working
                                                  mechanism
is a question of temperature regulation.
One is warned never to burn bridges, either real or metaphorical.
Keeping one's cool is a first principle in polite company.
And it is basic to our shared experience
that an overcooked egg becomes an art installation.
Einstein, an American émigré, won the Nobel Prize not for his
                                         work on relativity,
but for a study of the photoelectric effect, a study of light, of heat.

Every time I burn my fingers changing a light-bulb,
                                                it occurs to me that--
because sixty-watts of light produce seventy-seven degrees
                                               of ambient radiation,
two-hundred sixty degrees of surface radiant heat,
and over four-thousand at its vacuum core—
illumination is morally ambiguous.
Thus are we known to be characteristically ambivalent
                                           about Good and Evil
but fastidious on the question of Hot and Cold.

At some point, someone, presumably, must turn the machine on,
a gesture of anticipatory grace, nostrums sweeping over the altar,
an entire aesthetic of desire held in flux in the circumference of
a colossal zero buried under the cathedrals of ancient Europa.

If we are to glimpse something numinous lost to numerical
puzzles, taking up the timeline in a coil around the hand,
                              under the elbow,
the cosmological extension cord put away, then I want to see
                              what Icarus sees
in the instant just after his wings dissolve but before he falls.
I want to record the discipline of sixteenth century paint
                              and Greek fantasy;
a family of many artists, and Pieter Bruegel the Elder who
signed his work with a misspelling of his own name.

At the sub-atomic level, I am watching myself composing
                              my signature,
the lurid and unseemly continuity of letters flowing out
of themselves, into the encoded space of a blank page.
I see unmappable shorelines of identity looping endlessly
around the alphabet, reeling through catalogs of imperfectly
dotted i's, blind concessions to fate over and over without irony,
the vague memory of breakfast with a stranger under a hastily
                              scribbled sun or
telephone doodles dutifully retraced,
forever if necessary,
until I get it right.

Acknowledgements

I wish to thank the editors of the fine publications and projects in which many of these poems, sometimes in a different form, first appeared:

E• ratio

9th St. Laboratories

Chapbook, Vol. I

Zafusy

Referential Magazine

Birmingham Arts Journal

Drift Hermétique

Gennessee Word Lab

Heal Box

Xstream

I wish also to thank Johnny Summerfield, Melissa Dickson, Aaron Sanders, C. Stephen Foster, Tara McGhee, Beth Spencer, and Alan May for their sensitive and instructive readings of parts of this book. They are true masters of the Minotauric Arts.

A Note on the Art

Let me celebrate and humbly thank Joshua Jarrett for the beautiful and clever painting that became the primary source-image for the front and back cover. It seems Joshua had read my first book and was interested enough in the character of Felix Omega--who reappears, uninvited I might add, in this new text--to conceive him as a Post-Thesean, Neo-Noire, Fedora-wearing, Labyrinth-cartographer. I like that. And I like, too, that Melissa Dickson's design is both an exploration of those ideas as well as a gloss on Labyrinths themselves. No author should dare to dream of such lovely invention on the cover his books. I hope only that the poems within deserve the privilege of their splendid work.

Notes

Dream of the Labyrinth Semoiticians: The line containing the existential quantifier as the first letter of the word "Exit" points to a Badiouan notion of mathematics as ontology or, in this case, the ontological implications of Predicate Logic.

Pasiphaë with Baby Minotaur: An unusual depiction of the Minotaur in a domestic scene, of Etruscan origin.

Minotauric Equivocations with Shattered Referent Machine: The shattered machine is a scrambled fragment of source code for generating mazes.

L'infamï di Creti: The terza rima is from Canto XII of Allen Mandelbaum's excellent translation of The Inferno, in which Dante graciously gives the Minotaur a brief but chilling cameo as a languid harbinger of doom. In Taormina, Sicily the Piazza Duomo Square centers on a baroque fountain depicting the Minotaur in a heraldic scenario. Constructed some 300 years after Dante, the fountain begins to suggest the remarkable continuity of Labyrinth imagery in Western art.

Ten Sleeps and Topoi (Thesean Departures): The poetic narration here suggests that Theseus should map the Labyrinth in a Cartesian system. There are, of course, others that come to mind, in particular Curvalinear Coordinates, which would accommodate a rhizomic mapping of the Labyrinth's structure. Yet more compelling would be a Hamiltonian reading of the mapping problem. In general, Hamilton's spatial world is glimpsed through first-order differential equations but yield far more fascinating possibilities, not least among them the Sympletic Manifold, a speculative and dangerous geometric conception.

N(or): Delacroix never assayed the Minotaur explicitly, but his 1822 painting Dante and Virgil in Hell, known also as The Barque of Dante, seems fully conscious of the Minotaur's presence in the Dantean universe.

This is Only a Test: What is the Hadron Particle Collider but a postmodernist dream of Theseus, underground, framed by the twin delights of mystery and knowledge? Mythic forces are at work in the (Lab)yrinth of science.

www.ingramcontent.com/pod-product-compliance
Lightning Source LLC
Chambersburg PA
CBHW021019090426
42738CB00007B/825